# How to Improve Your Relationship with Your Sister

By Jean Young

EXPERIENCE
EVERYTHING
P U B L I S H I N G

## Disclaimer

This document is geared towards providing exact and reliable information in regards to the topic and issue covered. The publication is sold with the idea that the publisher is not required to render accounting, officially permitted, or otherwise, qualified services. If advice is necessary, legal or professional, a practiced individual in the profession should be ordered.

- From a Declaration of Principles which was accepted and approved equally by a Committee of the American Bar Association and a Committee of Publishers and Associations:

## INTRODUCTION

Having a sister means having a very special and unique relationship. She can be a friend or a rival. She can be an ally or an enemy. She can be the meanest person in the world to you but she can also become the best hero of justice when someone bullies you. Anyone who has a sister – blood-related or not – knows that having one is an emotional roller coaster. You can hate your sister one day and then love her the next.

In this book, you will learn how to maintain a good relationship with your sister. It is fortunate for you if you already have had a strong relationship with your sibling since you were young. However, that does not mean that you should be complacent and let things stay as they are. You have to show to your sister that you appreciate her.

It is also through this book that you will learn some techniques and advice to help you repair the broken relationship you have with he if that's the case. Not all sisters have good relationships with each other, after all. If you are not on good terms, then this book is the perfect self-help book to learn how you can have a strong relationship with your older or younger sister or sisters!

## HISTORY

The dictionary defines the word "sister" as a girl or woman who has the same parent or parents as you. However, that is not the only definition of a "sister". Someone who belongs to the same sorority or someone regarded as a comrade can also be called a "sister".

The term "sister" has an etymology stemming from the Old Norse word *systir*, which is consequently derived from the Proto-Germanic word *swester*. These are words that have the same meaning as "sister".

In studies, females actually display traits that indicate they are more jealous and competitive around their sisters compared to their brothers. In fact, there are cultures around the world that teach how sisters have the role of being protected by their brothers. The sense of protection coming from male older sibling is even stronger, especially in issues concerning bullies or advances from suitors.

Sibling rivalry between sisters is oftentimes stronger. There are even some that will last from childhood up until adulthood. Not every female is lucky enough to have her sister become her best friend, after all. It is more common for sisters to fight.

Improving the relationship between sisters should be an endeavor that everyone should go through. Your sister will always be your sister, regardless of what happens to you or what changes occur in your life. Nothing will change. Thus, aiming to have a good relationship with your sister is a must.

# CHAPTER 1 – SIBLING RIVALRY

## I. What Is Sibling Rivalry?

In the house with more than one kid, problems are bound to crop up. The younger sister might be jealous of how the older sister gets to do things that she is not allowed to do. The older sister might feel a disparity between the attention and love given to her and her younger sister. When sisters do not get along, you can call that sibling rivalry.

To break down the meaning of 'sibling rivalry', 'sibling' means a brother or a sister while 'rivalry' means competition. Establishing sibling rivalry with your sister is actually normal. If you consider your sister as a rival, you can drive yourself to work hard so that you can stand on equal ground or a level above your sister. You can be driven to be good at things that your sister is good at.

However, too much sibling rivalry can be unhealthy. You might lead an unhappy home life if the sibling rivalry is not properly resolved. Not only for you, you will also make home life difficult for the sibling you are having this unhealthy rivalry with as well as your parents. Moreover, bearing a grudge for a long time can fester your childhood. You should never allow sibling rivalry to eat you up as a person as well as ruin your relationship with a sibling who would otherwise become your best friend if you just learn to befriend her.

## II. Why Sisters Fight?

Many issues can pop up which lead to sisters fighting with each other. As sisters, there is a degree of competition and rivalry between the two so it is inevitable that they will clash and fight. The bickering and squabbling are parts of growing up with a sister.

### A. Common Factors for a Sibling Fight

Aside from competition and rivalry, there are other factors causing the sisters to bicker with each other. Here are some of the common factors why sisters squabble with each other:

1  Individual Temperaments. Each kid has individual temperaments (disposition, mood, and adaptability). Their unique personalities affect their temperaments and that also affects how they relate to their female siblings. For example, the younger sibling might be the type of child who is clingy and requires attention. The older sister, who might have a temperament of a responsible and reliable older sibling, might feel jealous toward the younger sibling since she wants the same attention too.

2  Evolving Needs. Children have their own needs, identities, and anxieties. These will definitely affect how these kids relate to each other. For example, school-age kids have the concept of equality so they might not easily understand why their younger or older sibling are getting more attention. Another example is when an older sister had developed a sense of being overprotective over toys and belonging. If the little sister comes along and takes away even one of her toys, she might end up becoming aggressive toward the younger sibling. For teenagers who have a concept of independence and individuality, they might not like it if they are held responsible for their younger sisters.

3   Role Models. The parents are always being mirrored by their kids. Thus, the parents must be the strong role models for the children. If the parents adapt a respectable and productive method for resolving conflict and disagreement, then there is a higher chance for the children to adopt those methods as well and be on good terms with their siblings.

**B. How to Say 'Sorry'**

When you have just engaged in an argument with your sister, you should not let it drag out for a long time. Unresolved arguments can no doubt lead to disconnection in support and communication. You will end up feeling alone, emotionally insecure, and isolated, especially if you previously have a strong emotional attachment toward the sibling you have just fought with.

Getting over the argument you had with your sister does not only mean moving on. This also means you are trying to get back the comfortable support of your special sibling relationship. You should take the initiative to repair the relationship with your sister.

Here's how you can say sorry to your sibling:

- Accept and show the feelings you have about the conflict. Your feelings are attached intrinsically to your behavior. Try to express your anger, anxiety, or frustration openly. By expressing your feelings openly, you can process your feelings which can then give you the chance to become objective regarding your perception of the conflict.

- Forgive your sibling for whatever transpired between you leading to the conflict. Remember that forgiving does not mean you just have to let go of your resentment. This also means that you are relinquishing the need to be right. Stop holding onto your grudge since that can prevent you from taking a step forward.

- If you have social supports, reach out to them. They can be your family members, friends, or even co-workers. The social supports you have usually stick with you both through negative and positive experiences. Moreover, they can offer you with objective insights regarding the argument. An honest discussion with your support system, despite how painful their opinions can be, will definitely help you move on.

- Despite being in a fight, you should never do mean things to your sibling. It can be really tempting to treat your sister badly after a fight but that will just worsen the situation. Moreover, it can become more difficult for you to apologize later on if you act mean towards your sibling.

- If your sibling says something obnoxious or rude, just ignore it. Some siblings aggravate their sisters for no reason at all. Instead of answering to their taunts, ignoring them will take the fun out of the situation. In the long run, they will stop saying obnoxious things.

- Apologize. It is always necessary to apologize after a fight. Apologizing does not mean you are conceding your stand. It means that you are truthfully regretting the part you have played in the conflict. You can still stand on what your opinion is regarding the fight but you can apologize for what you did that hurt your sibling. When apologizing, be specific about what you are apologizing for and accept responsibility for the behavior you showed without placing a blame on anyone else.

### C. Take the Extra Mile

You can also take the apology a step further. You might want to take the extra mile in apologizing to your sister by doing something special. Here are some of the sincere acts that you can do to show to your sister you regret fighting with her:

- Write a note. The note will not exactly become the end of the conflict. However, it should be a proof to your sibling that you really care and that you are trying to apologize and make up. The note you make for your sister does not have to be a big one. Just point out the things that you are apologizing for.

- Sometimes, it takes a good talk to resolve the conflict. You can invite your sister to a cup of coffee or dinner. You can then talk with each other, especially regarding the conflict. Depending on the severity of the argument, you can resolve it through games or you might need to be serious with the conversation.

- Cook for them. There is nothing that can beat good food. If you know what your sister's favorite food is and you know how to make it, then get into the kitchen and wear your apron now. Whip up the dish and serve it to your sister. If you cannot cook though, you can either ask for help from your parents or you can just go out and buy them their favourite dish.

- Let them have what they want. If you always argue over the TV's remote control, then you can concede for once and let them have it. This can be one of the many ways you can apologize and make up with your sibling.

Just because you are bonded by blood with your sister does not mean that you can fight without apologizing. It does not matter if you did or did not start the fight, there will always be things you have to apologize for in a fight. Even if you are sisters, you have to treat the other party with respect. Apologizing to your sister after a fight will show that you respect your sister and that you truly care for her. You can keep a strong relationship with your sister if you know how to apologize.

### III. When to Get Professional Help?

Getting professional help is necessary when the sibling fight escalates to more than what you, your sister, or your parents can handle. If you do not want things to get any worse, then requesting for professional counseling is only natural. Here are the times when you should consult a professional regarding severe sibling rivalry:

1. It is affecting your or your sister's daily functioning.
2. It is affecting the family members psychologically, emotionally, or physically.

Even when the sibling fighting is not that severe but you may have questions regarding the rivalry you have with your sister, consulting with a professional can be extremely useful. They are the ones who can answer your questions, after all. It is also through them that you can determine whether or not you can gain something from professional intervention.

## CHAPTER 2 – SIBLING HARMONY

## I. What is Sibling Harmony?

Siblings fighting is normal. It is inevitable and is also a perfectly healthy way for you and your sister to maintain your relationship as well as make compromises. While you may still bicker and fight with your sister, you should always aim for sibling harmony.

Sibling harmony is when you and your sister gets along well. If you are getting along well with your sister, then you will most likely lessen the sibling rivalry between you two. Sibling harmony will make your home life peaceful. Your positive relationship with your sibling will also positively affect your interaction and relationship with the rest of the family.

It is not only you and your sister who should aim for sibling harmony. Your parents must also be aware of how important it is for sisters to get along well with each other. It might require you and your sister to talk with your parents to eliminate the source of sibling rivalry and promote sibling harmony.

## II. How to Develop Sibling Harmony

Sisters are not naturally eternally jealous with their siblings. They can learn to get along too. They can even become best friends – becoming the other person's confidante.

Even if there are challenges that come with maintaining a healthy relationship with your sister, it is definitely possible to establish sibling harmony. Both sisters must invest in the relationship though to help establish sibling harmony. When both sisters invested in a loving relationship, this will definitely result to friendship of a lifetime.

There are recommendations that can help strengthen the relationship between the female siblings. These recommendations promote sibling harmony. Here are those recommendations that are worth following if you want to improve your relationship with your sister.

## A. Recognize the Importance of Your Role

No one else can take on the role that you have in your sister's life. There is no one who can replace you as your sister's sister. You must take the importance of your role in your sister's life as seriously as possible.

You can positively influence your sister. Invest in your sister's life with encouragement, love, praise, support, forgiveness, truth, and inspiration. Avoid becoming the source of harmful emotions and hardships to your sister's life. Never act selfishly. Never inflict them with strife, mockery, ridicule, annoyance, bitterness, abuse, nor deception. The influence you invest in your relationship with your sister will leave an indelible mark in your sister's personality.

## B. Spend Time With Each Other

To deepen the relationship you have with your sister, it is only natural that you invest quality time. Try to find ways on how you can include your sister in your daily routine or weekly plans. You might even want to do specific activities together like playing tennis or eating out every Friday night. Consider working on at least one thing together too. If you have a common goal with your sister, then you can easily build a solid sibling relationship.

## C. Take Time to Communicate

No matter what kind of relationship you have with the other person, know that communication is always a key component. When it comes to the relationship you have with your sibling, communicating with the latter will help boost your relationship with each other. You should take the time to talk with each other if that's the case.

You can just ask questions from them. Listen to what they are talking about. Paying attention to what they are trying to say is a part of the communication process. The discussion may include activities at the church, in school, or even in the neighborhood.

## D. Appreciate Differences

As you grow up, you and your sister will show differences. The distinction will go beyond age but it will become more evident in terms of spiritual gifts, skills, talents, interests, personality, abilities, and even love languages. Accepting the differences allow you to mature. You can also learn to successfully relate to others if you accept the individual differences each one has.

There are cases when differences make people part ways. However, instead of making these differences become the reason to drive you and your sister apart, use it as a chance to grow. Do not be afraid of these differences. Embrace them, learn about them, and certainly learn from them. You could learn to look at how they see things by taking on some of your sister's interests.

## E. Be Patient

Living with other people means you are close to them all the time. It will be easier for you to see the other person's shortcomings and character flaws. On the other person's party, they will also see what aspects of yours need improvement. Sisters are more brutally honest regarding the matter of your shortcomings and flaws.

When you are confronted by your sister regarding the shortcomings and flaws in your character, do not take offense. Instead, you should bear with it. Practice patience and forgiveness so that you can avoid getting into conflicts. Take their opinion about your shortcomings and flaws seriously and aim to mature.

If you see your sister's shortcomings and flaws, you can confront them about it as well. Let them know that you are pointing out their shortcomings and flaws for their sake. Moreover, you should give them time to mature and learn. Do not just expect them to change their shortcomings and flaws overnight. It might take some time but your sister will definitely put effort into improving steadily.

### F. Resolve Arguments Quickly

It is inevitable for arguments to happen between siblings. If conflicts arise, do your best to resolve the conflict immediately and repair your sibling relationship without any delays. In fact, you might need to humble yourself. Admit and apologize if you are the one in the wrong. Even if you are not in the wrong, you still have to apologize for any hurtful words, actions, or attitudes during the conflict. Do what you need to do to repair your relationship with your sister.

In case it is your sister who has offended you and has come to ask for forgiveness, do not be stubborn. Accept her forgiveness as soon as possible. Avoid harboring grudges for a long time, especially if it is toward your sister.

### G. Thank God, the Universe or other Higher Power for Having a Sister

It was the "forces that be" that placed you in your family and it is also that same force which gave you a sister. A sister is a very special existence. That special existence can become a positive influence in your life. You should thank God, the Universe or the Higher Power you believe in that such a special existence was given to you.

As you build a stronger relationship with your sister, you will see more and more things that you can be thankful for. You will see how good it is to have a younger or older sister. You can also entrust any conflict you have with your sister to the higher power, trusting to work everything out.

### III. How to Strengthen Sibling Relationship

Maintaining and strengthening the good relationship you have with your sister is a must. Of course, there is still the ever-present sibling squabble and fighting. Such fights can spice up the relationship you have with the special existence you call your sister. However, your fights should never escalate to one that can ruin the good relationship you have.

Your good relationship can be strengthened or maintained with ease if you take the effort to do so. Being able to stay in a good relationship with your sibling is a blessing and you do not want anything to ruin that. Here are some great tips that you can take advantage of so that you can maintain or strengthen the relationship you have with your loving sister:

- Admit that you just want to have a closer relationship with your sister. By admitting to yourself that you are willing to maintain or strengthen your sibling relationship, you should be able to motivate yourself to work hard. It will not matter even when there is a fear of rejection if you are motivated to be on good terms with your sister.

- Leave the guilt behind. The things that happened in the past should remain in the past. If your sister has stolen a few coins from your piggy bank when you were ten years old, do not bring that up over and over again – especially when you are fighting. These childhood misdeeds should be forgiven already. Just leave them behind.

- Make an appearance to special events. Some important events in your sister's life require obligatory attendance. Examples of these important events are weddings, birthdays, graduations, and even Thanksgiving dinner. However, you should take the time to attend some non-obligatory event. If your little sister is participating in a rock band contest, watching her from the front row banging her head to the beat of the music and then proceeding to the backstage after the performance is definitely a good surprise. Your sister will feel that she is definitely important to you since you take the time to attend such events.

- Stop being the family snitch. When it comes to families, alliances and private confabs are common. Even stealth reconnaissance like those you see in spy movies happen when it comes to families. For siblings, behind-the-back gossiping often happen – be it with another sibling or with the parents. These acts can actually erode trust between sisters so you should stop telling on your sister.

- If you frequently tell on your sister, it is highly likely that your sister tells on you to your mother too.

- Always mind your manners. Petty manners can annoy anyone – regardless of whether they are your sibling or your friend. If you do not ask your friend if she has taken a bath for one week, why would you ask your sister that? No matter how close you are with each other, there are topics that are off-limits. Examples of topics that siblings usually tag as off-limits include grammar usage, weight, and choice of friends.

- Be text friends. Hours-long conversations with your sister are worth a treasure. By spending time talking with your sister, you are definitely forging a bond with her. However, there are other forms of casual contact that you can take advantage of to improve the relationship you have with your sister. Text messaging your sister while at work, commenting on her Facebook post, and even pinging them on your BlackBerry will show that you are a thoughtful sister to them.

- Fight typecasting. Typecasting is when you are shoved into a role by other people. Your family might have pegged you as a loose cannon, the responsible one, or the baby of the family. Regardless of how old you are now, these labels will still follow you. Some people are happy with these typecasts since they know exactly what is expected of them. On the other hand, there are others who do not really appreciate being typecast simply because it is too stifling for them. Acknowledge the fact that your sister may have already grown out of the label placed on her. If you acknowledge it, the waves will ripple and the family will see the same thing. In fact, they might also acknowledge you growing out of your own label.

- Stop being envious of other people's relationship with their sister. If your best friend has a sister as well and they always go out for a movie every Wednesday night, do not be jealous. If you are jealous of the tight-knit relationship these people share with their sisters, you will just be devaluing the relationship you have with your own sibling. When it comes to sibling bonds, there are different depths to it. Even siblings that group hug each other will have one or two who drops an elbow. You have to remember this fact the next time you are jealous of another person's sibling relationship.

- Avoid the hot-button topics of religion, politics, and high-fructose corn syrup. What this means is that, when you are talking with your sister, you have to steer clear of topics that you are not on the same wavelength with. For example, you might think that being an atheist is okay but your sister prefers to be Christian. Instead of shoving one's religious belief in each other's throat, just stay away from that topic. That is just common sense. However, there are still a lot of people who forgets about this basic thing and so they always find themselves in hot water.

- When going for a family vacation, skip the spa. You cannot really bond together properly in the spa. Instead, you should aim to have at least two meals together. You also have to choose your own vacation destination and travel arrangements – perks of being an adult!

With these tips, you are sure to maintain the good relationship you have with your sister. Basically, think about what you do not want your sister do to you. Never do to your sister what you do not want her to do to you – the golden rule. Play nice if you want your sister to play nice too.

## CHAPTER 3 – BENEFITS OF HAVING A SISTER

### I. Why Having a Sister Is Good for You?

Indeed, there are numerous benefits that come with having a sister. By understanding what benefits you can get out of having a sister, it will be easier for you to accept them, establish a good relationship with them, and maintain that positive influence. The benefits your sister can bring to you will help you mature and grow as a person.

### A. Blood is Thicker Than Water

Blood is certainly thicker than water. This is an expression pertaining to loyalty and relationship within a family as the most important and strongest one.

There is a reason why this particular idiom exist. Even if you have never gotten along well with your sister in the past, you know that they will be there for you when you need them the most. After your friends have come and gone, the ones who will stay with you longer and until the end of the line will always be your sister. There is no doubt about that.

### B. Perspective Check

No one in this world will drag you back to reality, bring you back to earth, or put you in your rightful place faster than your sister. This is especially the duty of the older sister. If you are second guessing things about your life, you simply have to talk with your sister. They are the ones who take on the role as your living, walking, talking, and breathing perspective checks.

### C. Youth Lifeline

Your sister is your lifeline to your younger self. No matter how much closer you get to other people, it is your sister who knows you since childhood. She is the one who can tell your kids about how you act during your childhood, your pet peeves, or even your embarrassing childhood memories. It is also your sister who can verify the memories that you have, especially when you have forgotten something important from childhood.

### D. Stepping Stone to Success

Your sister will make it easier for you to get along with those people whose personalities are completely opposite to yours. This is a skill that will be extremely vital in the outside world. That skill will obviously help in your career. Through the experiences you have growing up with a sister, it should be easier for you to communicate with others more clearly, negotiate for the things you want or need, and even express your feelings. Fighting with your sister will also teach you how to stand up on your own.

### E. Sympathy Source

Having a sister makes you more selfless. It has been shown that having a sibling significantly improves the development of sympathy in a child. Quality relationships with sisters can promote altruism. Siblings actually rely on sibling affection to become a better person.

### F. Happy Meter

Individuals who have siblings are actually happier than those who do not have one. Forging a sibling bond and maintaining it over the years can become a lifetime of close friendship, endless amount of inside jokes, and emotional support. Those who are holding on to a tight relationship with their sisters actually lead a life filled with happiness as they grow older.

## G. Physical Fitness Promoter

Your sibling helps promote physical fitness. Your sisters will actually help you stay active. You can even engage your siblings to share a physical fitness exercise with you. By staying fit together, you can give a boost to your sibling bond.

## H. Mental Health Doctors

Well, not exactly doctors. Having a sister can mean that have you been spared during your "growing up" years from the feelings of guilt, fear, loneliness, self-consciousness, and lack of love. Your sister can give a positive boost to your mental health in a way that your parents cannot. Even if you are always fighting with your sister during your adolescent years, your sister is still protecting your mental health. For example, fighting can help you learn to control your emotions better.

## I. Long Life Medicine

Your sister can boost both your psychological health and physical fitness. Since that is the case, then you are guaranteed to live a long life. Also, the ties you have with your sister helps boost your longevity. Some reasons why you would live longer if you have a sister is that you might want to take better care of yourself for the sake of the loving sister and family members you have. When you are stressed out or sick, you have your sister to take good care of you too.

# CHAPTER 4 – A GOOD SISTER

## I. How to Be a Good Sister?

If you want to maintain or strengthen your relationship with your sister, then you have to become a good sister first. There are five significant qualities you have to cultivate so that you can be called a good sister by your sibling. Here are those five qualities you should adopt to become a sister your sibling can be proud of.

1. Loyalty – You have to become the person that your sister can count on. If you are a loyal sister, then you should stand by your sibling in all things. There might be times when you do not agree on some things your sister does or says but you still have to be loyal to her. Help her work through her issues and conflicts without abandoning her.

2. Honesty – Your sister will need to know that you are someone she can trust to be upfront with her. Honesty is a good thing but it can hurt your sister so you must be cautious before you say anything. Gently share your advice when you are asked about it. Have a keen eye to discern whether or not your opinion will become valuable when your sister did not even ask for it.

3. Trustworthy – Prove to your sister that you are a trustworthy sibling. People long to have individuals in their lives who they can truly trust. Your sister is of no exception. The best candidate your sister has is you. If your sister shares some relationship or personal problems with you, never share it with other members of the family (even your parents!) without asking for her permission first.

4. Good Listener – Being a good sister means that you also have to be a good listener. Your sister will most likely contact you when she needs to vent. Of course, she will also call you during treasured moments of their life. Your sister will need a person to hear her when she is exasperated, celebrating, hurting, or excited. You could take on the role of listening to your sister every time she needs to speak her feelings.

5. Compassion – It is tough to be compassionate with your sister all the time. This is especially true when you have given her advice on something and she didn't follow it, which resulted to the negative consequences she is facing. Such situations are actually the times when your sister needs your compassion the most. Do your best to respond kindly.

## CONCLUSION

If you are currently in the middle of fighting with your sister, reflect on the argument and see if it is really worth the cold or mean treatment. Your sister is someone important in your life and she is definitely someone you will need beside you in your lifetime. You should take the initiative to make peace with your sister and work on improving your relationship.

Making peace with your sister should not be a difficult task. When you have a fight, just apologize for the things you did wrong right away. Say sorry from the bottom of your heart. If you are sincere enough, your sister will definitely forgive you almost immediately.

If you are already in good terms with your sister, then you are fortunate. Make sure to treasure the sibling bond you have. It will become a treasure with a worth that is more valuable than diamonds. The good relationship you have with your older or younger sister is an irreplaceable bond.

Having a sister is definitely a blessing. As a takeaway, here are some points to remember:

1. Your sister will always be your ally.
2. Your sister is your best friend.
3. Your sister is important.

www.ingramcontent.com/pod-product-compliance
Lightning Source LLC
Chambersburg PA
CBHW071808020426
42331CB00008B/2440

*9 7 8 1 7 7 3 2 0 0 1 7 0 *